AN
EVERLASTING
GARDEN

A GUIDE TO
GROWING, HARVESTING, AND
ENJOYING EVERLASTINGS

JIM AND DOTTI BECKER

Interweave Press

The Everlasting Garden
by Jim and Dotti Becker

Design: Susan Wasinger, Signorella Graphic Arts
Photography: photos of all dried materials and photos on pages 12, 13, 16, 18, 21, 25,
26, 27, 28, 29, 30, and 31 by Joe Coca; background photo on cover by Dency Kane;
     other plant photographs by the author
Photo styling: Susan Strawn and Linda Ligon
Production: Marc McCoy Owens

 Interweave Press, Inc.
201 East Fourth Street
Loveland, Colorado 80537
USA

printed in Hong Kong by Sing Cheong

Becker, Jim, 1950–
     An everlasting garden / by Jim & Dotti Becker.
          p. cm.
     Rev. ed. of: A concise guide to growing everlastings. 1983.
     Includes bibliographical references (p. 93) and index.
     ISBN 0-934026-92-0 : $12.95
     1. Everlasting flowers. 2. Flower gardening. 3. Everlasting flowers—Drying.
     4. Everlasting flowers—Pictorial works. I. Becker, Dotti. II. Becker, Jim, 1950–
     Concise guide to growing everlastings. III. Title.
SB428.5.B43   1994
635.9'73—dc20   93-43316
                                                         CIP

First printing: 15M:394:CC

DEDICATION

We would like to dedicate this book to our parents,

Dorothy Dougherty and

Helen & Louis Becker

Today at Goodwin Creek Gardens, we grow more than a hundred varieties of plants for their dried flowers—and we're adding new ones every year. These plants are no more difficult to grow than other garden flowers, yet when we first decided to grow ever-lastings, we found little information to guide us and we suffered through many failures. The key, we have since learned, is not just knowing how to grow each plant, but more importantly, exactly when each one must be harvested.

The purpose of this book is to provide the information needed to grow and harvest fifty or so common everlastings. We have chosen these particular ones because they represent the wide variety of color and form, both as garden plants and as dried flowers, which is to be found among everlastings.

This book is divided into two parts. The introductory portion explains basic gardening techniques and terms within the specific context of these plants. This is followed by some general techniques for using these plants in dried floral designs. The second, and larger, section is arranged alphabetically by the plants' botanical names, and shows each plant in the garden as well as in its dried state. Here you'll find detailed instructions for growing and harvesting each one.

We hope that this book will give you the knowledge, confidence, and inspiration to add a few everlastings to your garden and to enjoy them throughout the seasons.

the Everlastings →

AN INTRODUCTION TO EVERLASTINGS

A YEAR IN OUR GARDEN

A garden has no beginning or end but is a continuous cycle of the seasons; there is something to do in every month of the year. It is the balance of growth and dormancy, hectic activity and relaxation, that sustains both the garden and the gardener.

Our quiet time is the dark month of December, when we sort and catalog our seeds and order any others that we will need. The excitement and anticipation of the new season begins as the old one has scarcely ended.

With the return of nice weather in January, we begin to tidy up the garden, raking leaves into the compost pile and removing branches blown down by winter storms. During February and March, we cut back the perennial plants and weed and fertilize all the perennial flower beds just as the plants are beginning to emerge from the ground. We start many of our perennial plant seeds in the greenhouse in late January, and the earliest of our annuals in March.

December brings dreams of fields of everlastings in a mountain meadow.

We begin to prepare our annual flower beds as early as the weather permits, generally in late March, but are often not finished until the first of May. The first seeds to go in the ground are those of poppy and larkspur in March, followed by nigellas, safflower, and starflower in late April and the amaranths in May. Perennials and hardy annuals that we have started in the greenhouse go outdoors late in April, followed by the half-hardy annuals in mid-May and the tender annuals in late May or early June.

June is the month for watering, weeding, and waiting. We begin to harvest our perennials in late June, and most have finished blooming by the end of July.

The hardy annuals begin to flower lightly just as the perennials are ending, and the garden is at its peak of beauty now. By mid-July, all of the annuals have swung us into the hectic activity of nonstop harvesting. Harvesting, as well as watering and weeding, continues right up until October.

We begin making our dried flower wreaths and arrangements as soon as a wide variety of flowers becomes available and continue this activity throughout the year.

Meanwhile, as each kind of plant ends its flowering cycle, we cut it back (if it's a perennial) or till it under (if an annual) and plant a winter cover crop in each fallow bed. Then as the rains of autumn begin and the frost nips the plants, we settle in for another winter and begin again our preparations for spring.

A field of strawflowers (*Helichrysum bracteatum*), and a few dried blossoms.

WHAT ARE EVERLASTINGS?

Botanically speaking, everlastings are a tribe of plants (the Inuleae) in the sunflower family (Compositae or Asteraceae) that have chaffy, papery bracts surrounding their flowers. These bracts, though petallike in appearance, are actually specialized leaves. In this book, however, we will call everlastings any plant species, regardless of its family ties, which dries readily when harvested while retaining its form and color. "Dried flowers" include the colorful bracts surrounding insignificant flowers, and the seedpods that remain after flowers have matured, as well as the flowers themselves.

This book is by no means exhaustive; it includes the everlastings that we happen to grow and grow well. You'll find a number of old favorites plus a few newer additions, such as larkspur and Blue Bedder sage, that retain vivid color with little effort. For additional listings, refer to the chart on page 92.

Botanical names are the only accurate and universal means of identifying different plant species. According to botanical nomenclature, every plant species has only one correct name, and no two species can have the same name. This is not true about common names, wherein two completely different species may both be called baby's-breath (*Achillea ptarmica* and *Gypsophila paniculata*) or a single plant species (*Lunaria annua*) may be called honesty by one person and money plant by another.

Each type of plant deemed by botanists to be distinctly different from all others is designated as a species. The name of each species consists of two basic parts, the generic name and the specific name, for example, *Lunaria annua*. The generic name, always first and always capitalized, is given to a group of species (the genus) that are in some way related and have certain characteristics in common, like the surname in human families. The generic name has meaning when used by itself. For instance, the genus *Lunaria* comprises three species native to Europe that have in common dry, translucent seedpods separated by a glossy white membrane. It is also proper to refer to these species as the lunarias.

The specific name (*annua* in our example above) serves to differentiate each and every plant in the genus (*Lunaria*) from all the others. There are three species of *Lunaria* but only one *Lunaria annua*. (In ordinary text, the second and succeeding mentions of a botanical name would be abbreviated: *L. annua*.) It is meaningless to identify plants only by their specific names, since plants of different genera can have the same specific name, for example, *Lunaria annua*, money plant, and *Artemisia annua*, sweet Annie.

A third botanical name is necessary to distinguish different varieties of a given species. This is especially important to gardeners as new varieties of cultivated plants are constantly being introduced. The varietal name follows the specific name and is preceded by the abbreviation cv. (for cultivar, or cultivated variety) or set in single quotes. Consider the white-flowered yarrow common throughout the United States, *Achillea millefolium*. Over the years, horticulturists have selected varieties of this species which have rose-pink flowers and have named two of them *A. m.* 'Rosea' and *A. m.* 'Rubra'.

Generic and specific names have their roots in the Latin language, and a translation of the name will often add meaning to the plant and its history. The generic name *Achillea* comes from the legend that the ancient Greek hero Achilles used the plant to stem the flow of blood from the wounds of his fellow warriors. *Millefolium*, "thousand-leaved," is descriptive of the finely divided, fernlike foliage. Cultivar names need not be Latin names, although those of the pink yarrows mentioned above happen to be Latin: 'Rosea' means rosy and 'Rubra' means red. Latin-English dictionaries of botanical names are available and are both informative and enjoyable reading (see Recommended Reading, page 94).

PLANT LIFE CYCLES

All plants are classified as either annuals, biennials, or perennials. Annual plants complete their life cycle of seed to plant to flower to seed and then die within one growing season. Biennial plants grow from seed to plant in one season and then flower and die in their second season. Perennial plants live for more than two years and usually flower during many growing seasons.

A woody perennial, such as a tree, maintains aboveground stems and sometimes leaves throughout the year. Herbaceous perennials do not have woody stems and in colder climates die back to the ground each winter. Underground stems and buds remain alive, however, and begin to grow again the following spring.

HARDINESS

Plants are also categorized by their ability to endure freezing temperatures. Tender plants can tolerate neither freezing temperatures nor frost. Half-hardy plants can withstand near-freezing temperatures and sometimes light frost. Hardy plants can withstand subfreezing temperatures; the extent varies among species and sometimes among cultivars of the same species.

WHEN TO PLANT

It is necessary to learn about the weather patterns at your garden site to determine the best times to place your plants outdoors. You need to know

**Opposite:
Statice loses none of its summer hue after being dried.**

the average yearly minimum temperature so that you can choose perennial plants that will survive the winter. This information has been compiled by the National Weather Service and the United States Department of Agriculture (USDA) and is available in most libraries. We have included the USDA Hardiness Zone ratings in the descriptions of perennial and biennial plants.

It is also important to know when the last frost is likely to occur each spring. Tender annuals must be planted after all danger of frost is past. You may plant half-hardy annuals after the danger of heavy frost and subfreezing temperatures is past, usually two weeks before the last probable frost date. Plant hardy annuals as early in spring as the weather permits, as early as four to six weeks before the last probable frost date.

Information on the last probable frost dates for your area may be available at your library, but it is often unreliable, as the conditions which promote frost formation can vary greatly within a very small geographic area. The best way to determine the last frost date is to make your own careful observations of the garden site and refer to published information only as a rough guideline.

After you have determined when to place plants in the garden, you can backtrack to determine when to sow the seeds of each species that you will be starting from seeds. As a rule, annuals need six to eight weeks from the date the seeds are sown until the young plants are large enough to transplant outdoors. Because biennials and most perennials will not bloom during their first year of growth from seeds, it is not crucial when you sow them. Any time during spring is fine.

Growing statice as a row crop is efficient and visually striking.

GROWING ANNUALS FROM SEEDS

All annuals, by definition, must be started each year from seeds. With a few exceptions (see Sowing Seeds Outdoors, page 16), we start all our seeds in a greenhouse and then transplant them outdoors when the weather is suitable. This gives the plants a head start and extends their blooming season by as much as eight weeks. Also, the adverse effects of weeds and harsh weather on seedlings are greatly reduced when large, healthy plants are transplanted outdoors.

Because annual everlasting plants are often not available in nurseries, you may need to start your own. This is not difficult, provided that you

have 1) seeds (see Sources, page 94), 2) a soillike medium in which to sow them, 3) planting containers, 4) liquid fertilizer, and 5) an environment with adequate light and temperature.

A good medium in which to sow seeds must be sterile, that is, free from living things such as weed seeds or fungi. Sterility eliminates the competition from weeds and reduces the likelihood of seedling diseases such as damping-off. The medium should readily drain off excess water but also hold moisture evenly and not dry out too quickly. It must be fine enough to allow small seedlings to emerge easily through its surface but firm enough to hold both seeds and seedlings in place during watering.

Garden soil is sometimes used as a seed-sowing medium, but we don't recommended it because it is highly unsterile. Although it is possible to sterilize any soil using either heat or chemicals, it is far easier to purchase an already sterilized medium at a garden center or variety store. Not all mixes are suitable for starting seeds, however. Some contain large chunks of material, such as tree bark, which would smother small seedlings. Some may contain chemical fertilizers, often visible as colored, sandlike particles, which can burn young seedlings.

We recommend a medium that contains perlite, vermiculite, and ground Canadian sphagnum peat moss. Such mixes are often called peatlite or soilless mixes, as they contain no garden soil. Perlite and vermiculite are naturally occurring minerals that have been expanded at extremely high temperatures to make them sterile and light in weight. Perlite is quick-draining, while vermiculite is very absorbent. Peat moss is a brown, fibrous material of plant origin which is mined from peat bogs. Although peat moss is not completely sterile, it is unlikely to contain any weed seeds or plant disease organisms.

Pegs spaced evenly in a board make it easy to seed flats uniformly.

We make our own peatlite mix using equal volumes of these three ingredients. Because peat moss is highly acidic, we add seven tablespoons of dolomitic lime to each bushel (about 3/4 tablespoon per dry gallon).

Although each plant species has optimal light and temperature requirements for the germination and growth of its seeds, most will do quite well under average conditions. A greenhouse is the ideal place for growing plants, but a sunny window can provide enough light for a few containers of seeds. All of the annuals in this book will germinate when temperatures are 60–75°F during the day and 50–60°F at night, temperatures easily achieved in many homes.

Any clean, sturdy container about 3 inches deep that drains water easily can be used for germinating seeds. A standard nursery flat measures roughly 12 by 18 by 3 inches and provides enough space to grow about a hundred plants. Flats are most often constructed of wood, plastic, or pressed plant fibers, but we find that flats made of fiber allow the peatlite mix to dry out too quickly.

PLANTING THE SEEDS

The procedure for planting seeds in flats is simple. First, thoroughly moisten the peatlite mix by mixing water into the medium with your hands or a shovel. When properly moistened, it should form a rough ball when squeezed in your hand, but it should not be soggy. Next, fill the flats with the moistened mix, taking care to fill all of the corners and eliminate air pockets. Level off the top of the flat with a straightedge and then firm the soil down to within 1/2 inch of the top of the flat.

Next, make rows of evenly spaced holes in the surface of the medium using either a pencil or sharpened pegs set at even intervals in a board. The holes should be 1½ inches apart both within and between the rows, and as deep as twice the diameter of the seeds.

Place the seeds in the holes and cover the surface of the flat with a thin layer of peatlite mix. To ensure that the planting holes contain no air pockets, draw the added layer gently back and forth across the tops of the planting holes with a straightedge. Firm the peatlite mix again and water the flat thoroughly. Water it often enough to keep the peatlite mix moist but not soggy and never allow it to dry out.

The number of seeds to plant in each hole varies with the plant species.

For example, the germination of acroclinium seeds seldom is less than 90 percent, and so one seed planted in each hole is sufficient to produce a good stand of seedlings. By contrast, that of orange globe amaranth seeds, under our growing conditions, is seldom better than 70 percent; thus, we sow two seeds per hole to produce a full flat of seedlings. When the seedlings emerge, thin them if necessary to one per hole.

Sow very fine seeds, such as those of yarrows, in rows rather than holes to avoid covering them too deeply with the peatlite mix. Space rows $1\frac{1}{2}$ inches apart, cover with a very fine layer of mix, and then firm and water the mix. Thin seedlings to stand $1\frac{1}{2}$ inches apart in the rows.

When seeds of a plant species are in short supply, it is wasteful to throw thinnings away. Instead, sow the seeds relatively thickly but evenly in a small container and then transplant all the seedlings into a larger flat when they have three or four true leaves. Prepare a flat of peatlite mix as if for seed sowing with rows of holes $1\frac{1}{2}$ inches apart and deep enough to accommodate the roots of the seedlings. You may tease them apart with a kitchen fork, taking care to disturb the roots as little as possible. Always handle a seedling by a leaf, never by the stems or roots. Hold a seedling in a hole with one hand while the other hand covers its roots with extra peatlite mix and firms it gently around the stem of the plant. The seedling should stand slightly lower than it was in its previous container. Water the flat immediately after filling it and keep it out of intense sunlight for several days.

A flat of acroclinium (*Helipterum roseum*) two weeks after sowing.

GROWING THE SEEDLINGS

After you have planted and watered the flats, place them in the sunlight; the seeds of most everlastings will germinate within two weeks. When the seedlings first appear, they will have a pair of thick, rounded seed leaves. At this early stage of development, they may be sensitive to the intense heat of full sunlight. If they show any signs of wilting, place them in partial shade for several days.

The emergence of the first true leaves is a sign to begin weekly applications of a liquid fertilizer. Because a peatlite mix contains few nutrients, the fertilizer must contain all of the nutrients necessary for plant growth. We prefer a mild water-soluble fertilizer. Follow the manufacturer's instructions carefully: improperly diluted fertilizers can badly damage even mature plants.

If the light and temperature are adequate, the seedlings will grow stocky and strong. Spindliness often indicates that there is inadequate light, the temperature of the room is too warm, or the plants are too crowded.

HARDENING OFF

A flat of seedlings of annual statice (Limonium sinuatum) promises bountiful color later in the season (above).

Seedlings and mature plants that have been raised indoors must be acclimatized, or hardened off, before they can be safely planted outdoors. This step is necessary for hardy plants as well as tender ones. A cold frame, which is basically a small unheated greenhouse with a lid that can be opened for ventilation, can provide the perfect conditions for hardening off: a cooler environment with shelter from frost, wind, and extreme cold. Open the lid during the day and close it at night. (Temperature-activated openers are available to tend it while you're away from home.) If a cold frame is not available, you may place the flats outdoors each day in a sheltered spot and bring them back indoors each evening. Plants should be ready for transplanting after ten days.

SOWING SEEDS OUTDOORS

We sow the seeds of the following annuals directly outdoors, as their seedlings do not always grow well after being transplanted: amaranths, ornamental grasses, nigellas, larkspur, poppy, safflower, and starflower. Prepare the soil well before planting so that the surface is smooth and fine-textured. Safflower seeds are large and can be planted in holes spaced about 8 inches apart. Those of the other species are best sown in rows. Water them immediately after planting and never let them dry out. Thin seedlings according to the distance specified for each species.

GROWING PERENNIALS FROM SEEDS

For a small garden, it is easier to purchase one or two of each perennial plant than to grow them from seeds. Plants of many perennial everlastings can be obtained through local or mail-order nurseries. Because many nursery workers are not well acquainted with the plants that they sell, verify the plants' botanical names to avoid a case of mistaken identity.

For most perennial plants grown from seed, follow the procedures outlined for starting annuals. The seeds of sea hollies and lavenders need to be moist-chilled, or stratified, to break their dormancy before they will germinate. As an approximation of winter, sow the seeds, moisten them evenly, and keep them between 32° and 45°F for two months. When you then expose them to temperatures of 60–70°F, the seeds will germinate. You may place the planted seed flat outdoors in a sheltered spot, such as a cold frame, and then move it indoors at the end of the chilling period; or put the flat (or a smaller container) in a refrigerator for the required period. Don't let the seeds dry out or expose them to extremely low temperatures.

Where winters are severe, wait until nearly springtime before placing the flat outdoors.

PROPAGATING PERENNIALS

After perennial plants have been in the garden for two full growing seasons, they can be increased in number (propagated) asexually, that is without seeds.

Many of the perennials in this book can be easily propagated by division in the early spring when the plants are just emerging from the soil. Lift the plant out of the ground with a spading fork and gently remove the soil from its roots. Cut off new shoots with some roots attached with a sharp knife and replant them in the garden or, if too small, in pots temporarily. If you bring these potted plants indoors to grow larger, you'll need to harden them off before transplanting them back into the garden.

Some perennials, particularly baby's-breath, oreganos, lavenders, and sages, are best propagated from stem cuttings, 3- to 4-inch-long prunings taken from the tips of nonwoody, nonflowering stems, usually in mid- to late summer. Remove the lowest two pairs of leaves from each cutting with small, sharp shears and recut the end to just below the point where the lowest pair of leaves was removed. Dip the end into a rooting hormone (available at garden stores), tap off the excess, and insert it about 1/2 inch deep into a pot or flat filled with a rooting medium. We use a mixture of 80 percent perlite and 20 percent vermiculite, moistened and firmly packed into the container.

Space cuttings about an inch apart and pack the medium firmly around each one. Water the medium immediately and keep it moist but not wet.

Cuttings root best when the medium is between 60° and 80°F. If you need to apply artificial heat to maintain this temperature range, consider buying a propagating mat, a waterproof electric heating pad that is placed under the containers. The mats are quite efficient because they put the heat only where it's needed, into the rooting medium. Propagating mats are available at garden stores or through specialty catalogs.

Keep containers of cuttings out of direct sunlight and wind. If the cuttings wilt a bit, mist them occasionally. Most cuttings will root within four to six weeks. New leaf or bud growth is a sign that rooting has occurred. Gently separate the rooted cuttings and transplant them into small pots. Keep them indoors in a sunny spot for three to four weeks and then harden them off before transplanting them outdoors.

Cupid's-dart and the sea hollies can also be propagated by root cuttings. Just before the new growth emerges in spring, lift a plant out of the ground and pull off some pencil-thick young roots without shoots. Prepare a flat of seed-sowing medium and level off its surface 1 inch below the top of the flat. Cut the roots into 2-inch sections and lay them on the surface of the peatlite mix. Cover them with 1/2 inch of mix, firm it, and water them. Place the flat in full sunlight and keep the peatlite mix evenly moist. When the cuttings produce new shoots and roots, you may transplant them into small pots and grow them for two or three weeks indoors. Then harden them off and transplant them into the garden.

SOIL PREPARATION

Soil is the thin layer of the Earth's surface that supports plant and animal life. It is made up of minerals, organic matter, water, air, and living things. Soil is the medium that holds a plant in place and provides it with the nutrients and water that it needs to grow. A good garden soil, like a seed-sowing medium, should hold moisture and nutrients but must drain excess water readily. It must be firm enough to secure the plants and to resist erosion but loose enough to allow roots to grow and air to circulate.

A field of annual statice (Limonium sinuatum).

Plants require sixteen elements for proper growth. Three of these are supplied by air and water, and the other thirteen come from the soil. Three of these thirteen elements are required in relatively large quantities. They are nitrogen, phosphorus, and potassium, represented by the symbols N, P, and K, respectively. The other elements are needed in much smaller amounts, but all are necessary for growth. A productive soil will contain all of these elements roughly in the proportions in which they are needed.

The amount of each element present in the soil can be accurately measured by a soil test. All states have a soil testing laboratory, which is usually located at one of its state universities. You can obtain information about these facilities at county or state agricultural offices or your local library. The results from a soil test will tell you how much of each element to add to make your soil more productive.

The test will also measure the pH, an indication of the soil's acidity or alkalinity. Most plants will do well in a slightly acid soil, but there are exceptions. The soil can be made more acid or alkaline in a relatively small area to suit the needs of specific plants. The soil test results will include recommendations for the materials needed to change the pH, or you can find them in a comprehensive gardening book.

The amount of each element that a plant needs depends primarily on the species but also on water, sunlight, and temperature. Many elements are abundant in the soil and required in such minute amounts that there is no need to add them to the soil. Most fertilizers emphasize N, P, and K, but it is important to remember the necessity for all of the elements.

Everlasting flowers have a reputation for being able to survive in poor soil, but our experience has shown that they are much more productive in a good soil such as that used for growing other flowers and most vegetables. The ideal soil should have N, P, and K in roughly the ratio of 3 to 5 to 3. A fertilizer formulated with this ratio contains 3 percent nitrogen, 5 percent phosphorus, and 3 percent potassium. One hundred pounds of this fertilizer contains three pounds of nitrogen, five pounds of phosphorus, and three pounds of potassium. A general recommendation for everlastings is five pounds of a 3-5-3 fertilizer per 100 square feet of garden area. Some plants have different requirements, and their needs are discussed in the growing instructions for each one.

There are two basic schools of thought concerning how the soil should be prepared and the garden as a whole maintained. The organic method uses only naturally fertilizers and stresses the use of gardening practices which will add organic matter to the soil. Organic gardeners also shun the use of chemicals to control insect pests and weeds. The inorganic method uses chemically produced fertilizers and often recommends the use of chemical pesticides and herbicides. Many gardeners use aspects of both methods.

We have chosen to grow all of our plants organically not only for what we feel are valid horticultural and health reasons but simply because it is the only natural way for us to garden. It brings us closer to the cycles of life and allows us to be more a part of our garden rather than apart from it. We strongly urge that you think carefully about which gardening practices to use. They must meet not only the needs of the plants but yours as well.

Whatever methods of gardening you follow, apply them thoroughly. A good garden soil should be prepared to a depth of at least 14 inches, and many perennials will grow better in an even deeper soil. Take care that the soil is well fertilized and of an even texture before it is time to set the plants into the garden.

TRANSPLANTING

The objective of transplanting is to set the plants into the ground with as little interruption of growth as possible. The soil should be well prepared and the plants hardened off and of the proper size. A plant with three pairs of true leaves is usually large enough to transplant. Some plants, particularly those with taproots, are better transplanted when they are a little smaller, as

their roots are less likely to be damaged.

Water the seed flat so that the peatlite mix is firm and adheres to the roots without crumbling, then cut the soil between the plants with a sharp knife, leaving each plant with a little cube of roots and peatlite mix.

Transplant the plants into the garden soil in the same way in which you transplanted seedlings into flats (see page 15). Cover the peatlite cube with garden soil so that it won't dry out more quickly than the soil surrounding it. Water the plants thoroughly after transplanting them. An application of liquid fertilizer at this time is beneficial. It is important to keep the top few inches of soil evenly moist (not wet) until the plants begin to show signs of new growth. Then begin watering less frequently but more deeply.

The loss of roots during transplanting is unavoidable, reducing the plants' ability to absorb moisture and making them more likely to wilt in the wind and sun. If possible, transplant plants on a calm, overcast day or in the late afternoon. If the plants do wilt, shade them with cheesecloth for a few days.

WATERING THE GARDEN

Water in the soil surrounding a plant's roots is necessary to carry the nutrients (in solution) to the plant and is itself a substance required for plant growth. Where the natural rainfall is insufficient to supply the plants' needs, water must be applied artificially.

How much and how often to apply water to the garden depend on the soil, the slope of the garden, the weather, and the plants being grown. In general, water when the top 2 inches of soil is dry. Apply it thoroughly so as to increase the time between waterings and to encourage the plant roots to grow deeply into the soil. A deep root system will give the plants a larger reservoir from which they can draw both water and nutrients.

Plant roots need oxygen as well as water. Too much water, as evidenced by a soggy soil and long-lasting puddles, will force out the air from between the soil particles and harm the plants.

Water can be applied by either soaking or sprinkling. Soaking—running the water into irrigation furrows or using drip irrigation systems or soaker hoses—puts the water directly into the ground around the plants. Very little water is wasted when a soaking system is used, and there is no risk of water damage to mature flowers.

Sprinkling sends the water into the air before it falls down onto the plants and the soil. Sprinkling is beneficial to plants because it increases the humidity around them and washes the dust off their leaves. For these reasons, we have found sprinkling to be the best watering system during our hot, dry, rainless summers. However, some water is lost into the air and onto nonproductive parts of the garden, such as pathways.

A sprinkling system must meet two requirements. The spray of water must be so gentle that it does not beat down the more delicate flowers, and the system must be able to supply the necessary amount of water in only three or four hours so that the flowers can dry off before nightfall. Many flowers, especially annual statice and baby's-breath, become discolored if they remain wet overnight. To prevent this problem, we pick off all mature flowers before turning on the water, and we recommend watering early on a sunny day so that the plants can dry off quickly.

The use of mulch with either system helps to maintain even soil moisture and reduce the amount of water lost by evaporation. Choose mulching material that is free of weed seeds. Keep it away from the stems and don't use it at all around plants that are susceptible to root or stem rot.

INSECT AND OTHER ANIMAL PESTS

We have not found everlastings to be any more or less attractive to insects than other garden flowers. Common insect pests such as aphids, spittlebugs, cucumber beetles, and various caterpillars have all appeared in our garden but have not caused serious problems. If you check your plants frequently, you can spot infestations before they get out of hand and eliminate them by simple measures such as hand picking the pests or mild organic sprays.

Deer, porcupines, and gophers are strongly attracted to certain everlastings and can be a real nuisance. Porcupines will pass up many a vegetable treat to dine on the succulent young flower buds of annual statice. Deer are fond of annual statice, amaranths, globe amaranths, sea hollies, and baby's-breath. Gophers will destroy many of the plants with succulent roots, such as sea hollies, cardoon, and Cupid's-dart.

DESIGNING AN EVERLASTING GARDEN

The sample garden plan on page 24 combines most of the plant species mentioned in this book in a compact, practical, but decorative design. It should provide more than enough flowers to use for gifts and home decorations.

If you prefer to create your own design, start by making a list of the plants that you want to include. Next, look up the recommended planting distance for each one. Plants of annual statice, for example, which are spaced 12 inches apart, each need a growing area of 12 by 12 inches, or 144 square inches. Grab your calculator and figure out the number of square inches required for all the plants on your list. Divide this total by 144, the number of square inches in a square foot, to give you the number of square feet you'll need to accommodate them all.

Sketch your design on paper, trying out different configurations if you like but always maintaining the same total area. Keep in mind that a practical everlasting garden is harvested frequently. Make the width of the design narrow enough so that you can easily reach all of the flowers.

Most everlastings prefer full sunlight. If you are planning to place the garden against a wall, hedge, or building, it must face south or at least southeast or southwest and have a minimum of six hours of direct sunlight each day. In arranging the plants, place the taller ones on the north side of the design so that they don't shade the smaller ones throughout the day. Try to visualize the effects of different floral color combinations and the placement of one plant's profile in front of, or next to, another's.

In our garden plan, we placed most of the annuals and perennials in

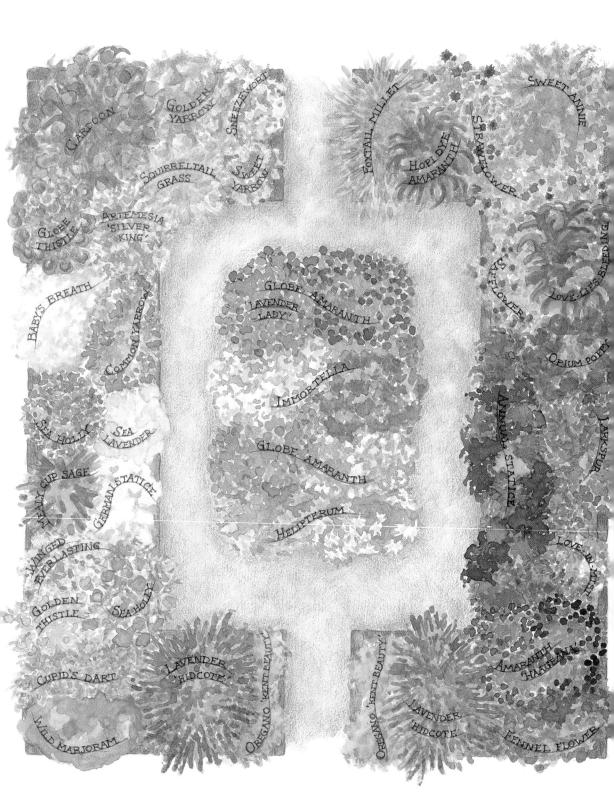

Even a small plot can provide enough everlastings for a season of dried arrangements.

separate areas to make it easier to prepare the soil for the annuals each spring and plant a cover crop or heavily mulch the annual area for the winter. Watering, too, will be more efficient, as annuals in general require more than established perennials.

HARVESTING AND DRYING

Straw flowers (Helichrysum bracteatum) can be cut from their stems and dried on screens.

All of the flowers and seedpods described in this book will dry perfectly if harvested at the proper time. Determining when to pick a flower is not always easy, however, because a single flowering stalk often produces many flowers which mature at different times. You must then decide whether to pick each flower separately on a very short stem or many flowers, at various stages of maturity, on a single long stalk. The size of the flower head, the number of blooms each plant produces, and the length of the stem most practical for its intended use are some of the factors which we consider in making this decision. Detailed harvesting instructions given for each plant include our recommendations for the length of stem to be cut with the flower. However, these instructions are intended only as a guideline; don't be afraid to experiment with different methods to find the ones that are right for you.

Flowers must be free from moisture when harvested; most will discolor as they dry if they are picked when wet.

After harvesting the flowers, strip the stems of large leaves and rubber-band them into bunches of about twenty-five stems. Avoid crushing the flowers. You can rub off small leaves after the flowers have dried.

Flowers with stiff stems can be dried upright. Others must be hung upside down so that the stems will dry straight. A coat hanger makes a convenient holder for hanging bunches. Weak-stemmed flowers such as strawflowers are usually removed from their stems and must have florists' wire attached before the flowers dry, preferably immediately after picking.

The ideal drying area is dark, dry, airy, and warm—70–90°F. Flowers are dry as soon as their stems break with a snap. It is important not to overdry them as they may become unduly brittle.

**Most everlastings dry
well hung in small
bunches in a warm,
dark area.**

STORING DRIED FLOWERS

Dried flowers can be stored either as hanging bunches or in boxes. Because many flowers are susceptible to moth damage, we recommend storing them in boxes containing mothballs or an herbal moth repellent. Wrapping a few bunches of flowers together in a cone of newspaper before placing them in the box will prevent them from becoming entangled. Use a shallow box so that the accumulated weight of the flowers won't crush those on the bottom. Acroclinium and immortelle are too delicate for long periods of box storage, and these should be stored as hanging bunches.

The storage area, like the drying area, should be dark, dry, and warm but not hot. Dried flowers reabsorb moisture in a very humid atmosphere, and must then be rehung and redried before they can be used.

PRESERVING FLOWERS AND FOLIAGE WITH GLYCERIN

Glycerin is a clear, thick, sticky liquid which can be purchased at drugstores. Plants that absorb a solution of glycerin and water become preserved in a process analogous to embalming. The primary benefit of preserving flowers and foliage in glycerin is that they remain more pliable and are less prone to shattering, shriveling, and leaf drop.

Although all of the flowers in this book can be successfully air-dried, a few, such as baby's-breath, annual statice, winged everlasting, and globe amaranth, are more durable if preserved in glycerin. This can be an advantage for floral designs which are destined for some physical abuse, such as hair garlands. Starflower, which is a bit delicate even when properly air-dried, is virtually shatterproof after preservation with glycerin.

Glycerin is also useful for preserving leafy stems that do not air-dry well. Though not discussed further in this book, these include eucalyptus, Oregon grape, baptisias, and many conifers. The disadvantage of glycerin preservation is that it changes the colors of the materials being preserved. Stems and leaves often turn brown or black. Flowers usually retain their colors but appear duller. Water-soluble floral dyes mixed with the glycerin can add color to the preserved plants, but our preference for natural colors has kept us from experimenting with them.

Mix one part glycerin with two parts warm water. Stir vigorously and fill small cups with 3 to 4 inches of the solution. Cut the flower stems and immediately place the stem ends in the liquid. If some time has elapsed between harvesting and immersion, recut the stems before placing them in the cups. Place the containers in a dark, cool spot, as extreme heat or sunlight will dry out the flowers before they can absorb the glycerin solution.

Complete absorption takes between three days and two weeks. Add more solution to the cups to keep the level above the stem ends until the flowers are completely preserved. The flowers are judged ready when they remain pliable and have turned a uniform color. If you leave them in the solution longer than necessary, an oily glycerin film may develop on the flowers.

Remove the finished flowers and dry or cut off the wet stem ends. At this point, some growers recommend washing the flowers with clear water and then hanging them up to dry. We have not found this step to be necessary. You may reuse the glycerin solution remaining in the cups up to three times, but first filter it through a screen or cheesecloth to remove fallen leaves, insects, and other debris.

A season's harvest ready for crafting.

Store the preserved flowers as you would dried ones. Because they are so pliable, they tend to flatten out more easily. Follow the same precautions for moth prevention as for dried flowers.

TOOLS AND TECHNIQUES FOR MAKING FLORAL ARRANGEMENTS AND WREATHS

We have refrained from presenting detailed instructions for making specific dried floral designs. Many books on the subject are available, and besides, we have always felt that the best designs are the ones which come from your own preferences and inspirations. What we will do is explain all of the basic techniques and materials necessary for dried floral work so that you can proceed on your own with confidence.

You'll need some florist's supplies such as floral tape, wire, foam, and

clay. All of these are available at craft supply stores.

Floral tape is a thin, self-sticking tape used to wrap several flower stems together into a bunch or a single stem onto a false stem of floral wire or the strong natural stem of a species such as golden yarrow. Many dried flowers need to be attached to false stems for additional stem strength or length. The most frequently used wire sizes are 24 gauge for small flowers and 20 or 22 gauge for larger ones. Green enameled wire blends in with the colors of the natural stems.

To attach one or more stems to a false stem, place the flower stem(s) alongside the false stem so that they overlap by at least an inch. Place the end of a roll of floral tape just above the point at which the

The soft, grayed pastels of statice, lavender, oregano, echinops, globe amaranth, poppy seed cases, and nigella, combine charmingly in this informal grapevine wreath crafted by the authors.

stems begin to overlap. Next (this takes some practice), twirl the stems between your thumb and forefinger while feeding the tape in a tight spiral down over them. Stretch the tape as you wrap so that it will adhere properly.

In a dried floral arrangement, the flowers are usually freestanding in a container filled with a material that will hold the stems firmly in place. The most commonly used material is floral foam, which is sold under such trade names as Barfast or Sahara. It comes in dense blocks which can easily be cut with a knife and held in place with either glue, double-sided adhesive tape, or wire. Often you can jam the foam tightly enough into the container so that neither wire, glue, nor tape is necessary. Cover the foam with a loose layer of sphagnum moss to give a more natural appearance.

Floral clay is sometimes used in place of floral foam. This nonhardening clay is especially useful in filling small openings. It has the advantage of adding weight to the container, but it accepts stems less readily than foam and is more expensive.

Containers not only hold the flowers in place, but they add their own visual component to the arrangement. The choice of containers is strictly a matter of taste. Virtually anything can be used as long as it is stable and has an opening large enough to accept the flower stems. Containers can run the gamut from old shoes and hollow logs to traditional baskets, terra-cotta flowerpots, and copper bowls.

If the container is not heavy enough to keep the arrangement from rocking or falling over, you must add weight to it before making the arrangement. Sand or small pebbles work well as ballast. If the container is a basket, enclose the sand in a plastic bag to prevent leakage. Place the ballast in the bottom of the container, holding it in place with the floral foam or clay.

An alternative to using either foam or clay is simply to fill a leakproof container with fine-grained sand. Sand easily fills a container of any shape and adds weight, but it does not hold the stems as firmly as foam or clay does.

Before beginning your arrangement, consider its proportions, symmetry, and color combinations. Feel free to experiment with these elements of floral composition whenever you work with flowers. Use books for ideas, but always do what is personally pleasing, and above all, have fun.

Start by assembling the flowers you will be using. Next, define the height, width, and shape of the arrangement by placing in the container a few of the longer, more linear flowers such as larkspur and the artemisias. Gradually fill in the space, saving the smallest and brightest flowers for last.

When working with small individual flowers, such as those of globe amaranths and winged everlasting, you'll find it easier to bunch three or four together onto one wire rather than wire each one separately. You can also combine several different types of flowers onto one wire, which diffuses the colors throughout the arrangement instead of pinpointing them in small groups. As the arrangement becomes crowded with flowers, a pair of needle-nosed pliers comes in handy to insert new ones into the container.

A wreath is a wall arrangement in the round, with the backing serving as both the container and the material that holds the flowers in place. Wreath backings are typically straw or sphagnum moss bound tightly over a wire frame, or vines, stems, or branches looped and twined together into a circle.

Wreath backings are easy to make. You can purchase sphagnum moss and wire frames at craft stores, but you may have to buy straw by the bale

Several of the artemisias make handsome and versatile wreath bases.

Bunch several stems of small individual flowers together for easier handling.

GLOSSARY

BRACT: a modified leaf located just below the flower

CALYX (PLURAL CALYCES): the sepals of a flower; the outer circle of floral parts, surrounding the petals; may form a cup

COROLLA: the petals of a flower

DOUBLE: more than the usual number of petals, which are often crowded together

FLORET: a small flower which is part of a dense cluster

FLOWER: the reproductive structure of seed-bearing plants

from a farm supply store. Commercially made straw wreaths are readily available and inexpensive. Choose a wire frame that consists of two concentric circles connected by wire spokes to form a shallow trough between them. Pack this trough tightly with the moss or straw and hold it in place with green floral wire.

Twined wreath backings can be made from almost any plant that is long, strong, and flexible enough to be bent into a circle. Grapevines, willows, and several artemisias are commonly used. The artemisias are excellent choices because they are easy to grow and their leaves and tiny flower heads remain on their stems even after being dried. The silvery foliage of some species contrasts well with colorful dried flowers.

Twine a wreath backing while the materials are fresh, or they will become too dry and brittle to bend. Woody plants such as willow and grapevines are cut back while dormant. Vineyards usually prune their vines in late winter or early spring and are often happy to give away their prunings. Artemisias are harvested in late summer or early autumn, at the end of their growing season.

You'll need several stems to make a single twined wreath backing. Start with stems that are three to four times as long as the diameter of the desired wreath. For example, to make a wreath 10 inches in diameter, you'll need some stems at least 30 to 40 inches long.

Bend one of these stems into a circle, with the tip end overlapping the butt end by about 6 inches. Wrap the overlapping tip around the butt end in a tight spiral. Wrap a second stem completely around the circular form of the first one, also in a tight spiral. Repeat this procedure until you have a wreath of the desired thickness. As you add new stems, adjust the shape of the wreath so that it remains circular.

One drawback to using grapevines is that wild ones and even the prunings from some vineyards can be infested with the eggs of boring insects. They hatch into larvae that consume the pith of the vines, making considerable noise and mess. Commercially made grapevine wreaths usually have been treated to kill these eggs and larvae. At home, you can try boiling the wreaths in a large pot of water for several minutes and then drying them thoroughly before using.

Because wreaths are circular, some symmetry of form and color is necessary, but a wreath in which a pattern of flowers continues unvaryingly often looks contrived and uninteresting. A wreath backing that is intrinsically decorative, as the twined types are, need not be completely covered with flowers; highlighting a portion of it can be very appealing.

Begin decorating your wreath backing by wiring flowers into small bunches. As with tabletop arrangements, you can either wire together flowers of the same type or combine different types. We like our wreaths to have a bit of outward flare, so we usually bundle small, colorful flowers together with linear, neutral-colored ones such as the artemisias, sea lavender, and small lichen-covered branches.

The wires to which the flowers are taped must be long enough to pass through the body of the wreath backing. Twist the ends of these wires around the wire frame or the thicker twined stems. Take care that the wires are not visible from the front or sides of the wreath. You may need to use needle-nosed pliers to pierce the wreath backing with the wired bunches. Insert flower bunches all the way around the wreath. If the finished wreath appears out of round, trim off or add materials to restore its symmetry.

Dried floral designs will last for a least three to four years with proper care. All natural colors will fade slowly, but they will last much longer if kept out of direct sunlight. Direct moisture or high humidity will also hasten color loss and will cause some flowers to droop.

It is difficult to clean a dirty, dusty wreath or arrangement; don't let it get that way. Dust is easily removed by light, periodic blowings with a hair dryer set on cool. You can extend the life of a favorite design by replacing the most faded dried flowers by a few newer, brighter ones.

OVARY: the basal part of the pistil which contains the future seeds (ovules)

PETAL: one of the inner floral parts that encircle the reproductive organs of a flower

PISTIL: the female reproductive organ of a flower

POD: a dry seed vessel that may or may not split open when it is mature

STAMENS: the male reproductive organs of a flower that produce the pollen

STYLE: the tubular middle portion of the pistil

ACHILLEA SPECIES

HARDY PERENNIALS

PROPAGATION:
division, seeds
(A. ageratum,
A. filipendulina)

HEIGHT:
A. ageratum (20"),
A. filipendulina (60"),
A. millefolium (24"),
A. ptarmica (24"),
A. 'Moonshine' (20"),
Galaxy hybrids (24–36")

PLANTING DISTANCE:
A. filipendulina (18"),
all others (10")

FLOWER COLOR:
A. ageratum, A. filipendulina
(yellow), A. 'Moonshine'
(pale yellow), A. ptarmica
(white), A. millefolium and
Galaxy hybrids (shades of
rose, pink, red, or salmon)

FLOWERING PERIOD:
July–August

ZONES: 3–9

There are more than a hundred species of yarrows, and they vary greatly in size and flower color. Several are excellent everlastings.

Achillea filipendulina is the golden yarrow commonly found in gardens and floral shops. It is one of the largest yarrows, reaching a height of 5 feet, with round, flat yellow flower heads up to 5 inches in diameter. Like most other yarrows, its foliage is finely divided and fragrant.

A smaller but somewhat similar species is sweet yarrow, *A. ageratum*. Its stalks reach a height of 1½ feet, and its dense yellow flower heads are only 2 inches across. Its common name refers to the sweetish scent of the leaves, which are less divided than those of golden yarrow.

Rose and pink flowers can be found in several cultivars of *A. millefolium*, including 'Cerise Queen' and 'Fire King'. These plants have bright flowers and attractive, feathery foliage, but they spread rapidly by underground stems and can be troublesome if they are not contained by an edging material. Seeds, even those of named varieties, will produce offspring with a wide range of flower colors. The only way to obtain flowers of a given color is to purchase plants that are in bloom or those that have been propagated asexually from cultivars with proven characteristics.

Another invasive, though useful yarrow, is sneezewort, *A. ptarmica*. Its small white flower heads grow in loose clusters, and its leaves are linear and undivided. The best flowers for drying are those of the fully double cultivars such as 'The Pearl' because they dry pure white. Though seeds are available, the offspring are variable.

Several hybrid yarrows of relatively recent origin provide even further choices of flower color. These include 'Moonshine', pale yellow; 'Beacon',

A. filipendulina

A. ageratum

Achillea filipendulina and A. 'Moonshine'

bright red; and 'Salmon Beauty', salmon pink. The latter two are part of the Galaxy series, which are noted for their stout, upright stems and large flower heads.

Pick yarrows when their flower heads are firm to the touch. For *A. millefolium* and the hybrids, this is after the flowers have begun to fade. If picked earlier, when the colors are brighter, they will only shrivel when dried. Hang the flowers upside down to dry.

Yarrows require full sun and well-drained soil. Though established plants will tolerate drought, they do best in moist, fertile soil.

All varieties are easily propagated by division. *A. ageratum* and *A. filipendulina* may also be grown from seeds, with only slight variability among the offspring.

A. millefolium
'Rosea'

Achillea ptarmica

Achillea millefolium 'Rosea' and A. ptarmica

AMARANTHUS SPECIES

AMARANTH • LOVE-LIES-BLEEDING

PROPAGATION: seeds

HEIGHT: *A. caudatus* (36–60"), *A. hybridus* var. *erythrostachos* 'Green Thumb' (20"), *A. cruentus* 'Komo' (72")

PLANTING DISTANCE: *A. caudatus*, 'Komo' (12"), 'Green Thumb' (8")

FLOWER COLOR: *A. caudatus* (rose-pink), 'Green Thumb' (green), 'Komo' (maroon)

FLOWERING PERIOD: *A. caudatus*, 'Green Thumb' (August), 'Komo' (August–September)

The genus *Amaranthus* comprises annuals native to the tropics and other mild climates. They are often grown for their colorful flowers and foliage and their edible seeds and leaves. Many also are outstanding everlastings.

Love-lies-bleeding, *Amaranthus caudatus*, is a large, well-branched plant 3 to 5 feet tall with a stout red stem and reddish-green leaves. The rose-pink flowers are arranged on drooping, ropelike terminal spikes.

A smaller variety which provides an unusual green color for fresh and dried designs is 'Green Thumb', a cultivar of *A. hybridus* var. *erythrostachos* (formerly *A. hypochondriacus*). In contrast to many other amaranths, it grows in a stiff, columnar form to a height of just 20 inches.

A. caudatus

A. hybridus var. *erythrostachos* 'Green Thumb'

Amaranthus caudatus

Our favorite amaranth for drying is the Hopi dye amaranth, *A. kruentus* 'Komo'. The Hopi grow this variety for a scarlet food dye as well as for its edible seeds. It is an impressive plant, growing to a height of 6 feet, with deep reddish purple stems, bronzy purple leaves, and maroon flowers.

Pick amaranths when their flower spikes are at their peak of color but before they produce seeds and begin to discolor. If you cut the large terminal spike down to a new flower bud, a second crop of flowers will develop. Bunch the spikes and hang upside down to dry.

Amaranths can be started indoors and transplanted into the garden with some success, but they grow much larger when seeds are sown directly outdoors. They tolerate some drought but grow best in good, moist soil in a hot, sunny climate.

A. cruentus
'Komo'

Amaranthus cruentus 'Komo' and *A. hybridus* var. *erythrostachys* 'Green Thumb'

AMMOBIUM ALATUM

**HALF-HARDY
PERENNIAL**

PROPAGATION: seeds,
division

HEIGHT: 30"

**PLANTING
DISTANCE:** 10"

FLOWER COLOR: white

FLOWERING PERIOD:
July–August

ZONE: 7–10

Ammobium alatum is a common garden flower, and the cultivar 'Grandiflora' is the purest white everlasting that we grow. It must be grown as an annual where winter temperatures often go below 20°F. The plant forms a clump of basal leaves and produces many well-branched flowering stalks enlarged by membranous wings, hence the name winged everlasting.

The flower heads are 1/2-inch yellow buttons surrounded by numerous rows of white papery bracts. Flowers picked just as the white bracts have unfurled but before the yellow center appears will dry pure white. If picked later, they will dry with a yellow-brown center. Pure white flowers will have stems only about 6 inches long. If you allow all of the flowers on a stalk to open, you may pick them together on a longer stem. Hang them upside down to dry.

A. alatum

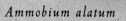

Ammobium alatum

ARTEMISIA SPECIES

WORMWOOD • MUGWORT • SWEET ANNIE

HARDY PERENNIALS,
ANNUAL

PROPAGATION:
division (*A. ludoviciana* and
cvs., *A. vulgaris*), seeds
(*A. absinthium*, *A. annua*,
A. vulgaris)

HEIGHT: *A. annua*,
A. vulgaris (72–84"),
A. ludoviciana and cvs.
(24–36"), *A. absinthium*
(60")

**PLANTING
DISTANCE:**
A. annua, *A. ludovicianus*
and cvs. (12"), *A.
absinthium*, *A. vulgaris* (18")

FLOWER COLOR:
leafy stems silver-gray or
gray-green, flowers yellow
or beige

FLOWERING PERIOD:
A. absinthium, *A.
ludoviciana*, and cvs., *A
vulgaris*–August; *A
annua*–September

ZONES: 4–9

There are more than 200 species of *Artemisia*, mostly native to the Northern Hemisphere, representing plants large and small, annual and perennial. Their leaves are usually divided, in some species quite finely, and are often an attractive silver-gray. Their flowers are clustered in tiny heads arranged in long, leafy spikes or panicles. Though the flowers of most species are not very conspicuous, the long, flexible, leafy stems, with or without flowers, are excellent material for wreath backings or tall floral arrangements.

A. absinthium is the common wormwood of herb gardens. It is a semiwoody shrub up to 6 feet tall with silver-gray leaves. The flower heads are pale yellow, and they will maintain this color on drying. Pick the long flowering stems at their peak of color, which is often just as their pollen is being released. Wormwood pollen can be an irritant, and we recommend wearing a good pollen mask available at pharmacies when harvesting large amounts of this herb.

Another herbal artemisia useful for dried floral designs is mugwort, *A. vulgaris.* It is an herbaceous perennial but quickly grows to a height of 7 feet each summer. It has purple stems and deeply cut leaves that are green above and silver beneath. Harvest stems just as the flowers are maturing. Mugwort spreads by underground stems and can become invasive.

A. absinthium

A. annua

42

Artemisia annua and *A. absinthium*

A. ludoviciana, a native of the southwestern United States, has nearly linear silver-gray foliage. The cultivar 'Silver King' has narrow leaves and thin, well-branched stems. 'Silver Queen' has broad leaves and thicker stems, and plants are less erect. Neither cultivar produces many flowers. Harvest stalks in late summer before the leaves begin to discolor. This species and its cultivars spread via underground stems.

A. annua, called sweet Annie or sweet wormwood, is highly fragrant and the only annual in this group of artemisias. It can easily top the others, however, with stalks growing rapidly to more than 7 feet tall. Some people are allergic to sweet Annie or dislike its strong scent. If you are among them, choose another of the artemisias for your floral designs. Sweet Annie may be picked when green or tan. In the green stage, it is often releasing copious amounts of pollen: wear a pollen mask when harvesting. It can also be harvested after the flower heads have released their seeds and turned light tan. If you pick sweet Annie at this stage, be aware that it self-sows readily.

Form the artemisias into wreath backings immediately after harvesting them (see page 30). If you plan to use them in tall floral arrangements or swags, dry them first by hanging the stems upside down.

Give artemisias a sunny position. *A. absinthium* and *A. ludoviciana* and its cultivars require a well-drained soil and cannot tolerate wet conditions. *A. vulgaris* and *A. annua* will grow almost anywhere but prefer good, moist soil.

A. vulgaris

A. ludoviciana
'Silver King'

Artemisia vulgaris and *A. ludoviciana*

CARTHAMUS TINCTORIUS

HARDY ANNUAL

PROPAGATION: seeds

HEIGHT: 24"

PLANTING DISTANCE: 8"

FLOWER COLOR: yellow or orange and green

FLOWERING PERIOD: July

Safflower is a plant of the Old World that has been in cultivation since ancient times. It has been an important source of dye since the time of the Egyptians and is increasingly grown today as an oilseed crop.

The species looks like a thistle, with smooth, thick stems and painfully spiny leaves. Spineless varieties have been developed and are a great improvement. Each plant is well branched and will produce several flower heads. Each flower head consists of many green leafy bracts which constrict around a tuft of yellow or orange florets.

Pick flower heads just as their florets are reaching their peak of color. Entirely green flower heads can also be useful in dried decorations; pick them before any florets appear. Both flower heads and stems are stiff and can be dried upright.

Safflowers are difficult to transplant, and so their seed is best planted directly outdoors (see page 16). Choose a site with well-drained soil, as plants are susceptible to root rot.

C. tinctorius 'Safflower'

Carthamus tinctorius

Catananche caerulea

HARDY PERENNIAL

PROPAGATION: seeds, division, root cuttings

HEIGHT: 24"

PLANTING DISTANCE: 10"

FLOWER COLOR: lavender (fresh), blue (dried)

FLOWERING PERIOD: July–August

ZONES: 3–9

The name Cupid's-dart refers to this plant's ancient use as a love potion. It is a hardy perennial native to the Mediterranean region and one of the few blue everlastings. The plant forms neat mounds of narrow leaves with many well-branched flowering stalks. Each plant may produce more than a hundred flowers during a single growing season.

The flower heads consist of many long, lavender, petallike ray flowers surrounded by a series of bristly, translucent bracts. As they dry, the "petals" shrivel and change color, forming a bright blue tuft. There are also white-flowered varieties which are lovely in the garden but do not dry well.

Pick the flowers when they are fully developed but before they begin to fade. Because they close before noon on sunny days, you'll need to check them early in the morning and pick them as soon as the dew has evaporated. Hang them upside down to dry.

C. caerulea

Catananche caerulea, picked after most of the blue ray flowers have faded

CENTAUREA MACROCEPHALA

HARDY PERENNIAL

PROPAGATION: seeds, division

HEIGHT: 36"

PLANTING DISTANCE: 16"

FLOWER COLOR: golden yellow

FLOWERING PERIOD: July

ZONES: 3–7

Golden thistle is a member of a genus that includes lovely garden flowers as well as tenacious garden weeds. It is a coarse but handsome plant with long, broad leaves and tall, thick flowering stalks bearing large flower heads 2 inches across. Each flower head comprises a tuft of golden yellow florets surrounded by a series of large, bristly bronze bracts.

By picking flower heads at different stages of their development, you can obtain three distinctly different dried flowers. The large, round buds have a slight resemblance to tiny pineapples, and the plant is sometimes called pineapple thistle. Our favorite way to harvest the flower heads is just as the florets are fully open, when both the bronze bracts and the yellow tuft are displayed. Flower heads picked after releasing their seeds resemble the closed buds but are larger and cuplike. Hang the flowers upside down to dry.

C. macrocephala

Centaurea macrocephala

CONSOLIDA ORIENTALIS

HARDY ANNUAL

PROPAGATION: seeds

HEIGHT: 36–48"

PLANTING DISTANCE: 4–6"

FLOWER COLOR:
white, pinks, rose, salmon, blue

FLOWERING PERIOD:
July

Larkspurs are frequently used as either dried or fresh cut flowers. They were formerly assigned to the genus *Delphinium*, and many seed catalogs still list them by that name.

The plants are moderately branched to a height of 4 feet and bear either single or double flowers of various colors. The uppermost sepal and petal in each flower form a long spur, and the name larkspur comes from the fanciful similarity of this structure to the spurclaw on the foot of the European lark.

Several series of cultivars with flower colors in white, pinks, and blues have been developed. These include Imperial and Messenger.

The flower stems on each plant mature over a period of several weeks. Harvest each stem just as the flowers lowest down on the stem are beginning to fade. At this time, the flower buds at the tip may be just slightly open. Hang stems upside down to dry and don't overcrowd the bunches as the flowers flatten readily.

Sow seeds directly outdoors either in the fall or very early in the spring, as they germinate best in cool weather. Because larkspurs are susceptible to various fungal diseases, avoid planting them in wet, poorly drained soils.

C. orientalis

Consolida orientalis

53

Cynara cardunculus

HARDY PERENNIAL

PROPAGATION: seeds, division

HEIGHT: 60"

PLANTING DISTANCE: 24"

FLOWER COLOR: purple

FLOWERING PERIOD: July

ZONES: 7–9

The cardoon, a close relative of the globe artichoke, is also edible, but the succulent portions are the leaf stalks, which are tied up and blanched before being harvested. It is a very large plant, with leaves over 2 feet long and flowering stalks 5 feet high. It is not hardy in cold climates and requires winter protection in areas where the temperature goes below 10°F.

Each plant produces several sparsely branched flowering stalks. The flower head comprises many spiny bracts surrounding a large tuft of bright purple florets. Pick the flowers as soon as the florets are fully open and at their peak of color. Hang the stems upside down to dry.

Grow this plant in a deep soil with abundant moisture and fertilizer as befits its enormous size.

C. cardunculus

Cynara cardunculus

ECHINOPS SPECIES

HARDY PERENNIALS

PROPAGATION: seeds, or division of plants more than three years old

HEIGHT: *E. bannaticus* (24–36"), *E. exaltatus* (60"), *E. sphaerocephalus* (84")

PLANTING DISTANCE: 18"

FLOWER COLOR: *E. bannaticus, E. exaltatus* (blue), *E. sphaerocephalus* (green)

FLOWERING PERIOD: July

ZONES: 3–8

The name *Echinops,* from an ancient Greek word meaning "like a hedgehog," aptly describes the round and spiny flower heads of this genus. Each spine is actually an individual floret comprising a blue or white corolla surrounded by a series of bristly bracts.

Only a few of the hundred or so species of *Echinops* are widely grown in gardens. The two most common ones are *E. bannaticus* (formerly *E. ritro*) and *E. exaltatus,* rough, coarse plants with large, divided, spine-edged leaves. *E. bannaticus,* which grows 2 to 3 feet tall, is the most suitable for small gardens. *E. exaltatus* can reach a height of 5 feet and has more sparsely branched flowering stalks and spinier leaves. The blue flower heads of these two species are similar, and the species are often confused in the trade.

A third species, *E. sphaerocephalus,* grows up to 7 feet tall. Its flower heads are similar to those of the above-mentioned species, but the floral bracts are a distinctive green.

Pick globe thistles when the bracts are at their peak of color but before the corollas emerge. Heads picked later will shatter easily. Because flower heads on a given stalk mature at different times, you must pick them separately on 2- to 6-inch stems. You may bunch them and hang them upside down or simply dry them loose in a basket.

The plants need a well-drained soil in a sunny location. They can tolerate drought but do best with moderate watering.

E. exaltatus

E. sphaerocephalus

Echinops exaltatus

ERYNGIUM SPECIES

HARDY PERENNIALS

PROPAGATION: seeds (require moist-chilling, see page 17), division (*E. planum*)

HEIGHT: *E. giganteum* (60"), *E. planum* (36")

PLANTING DISTANCE: 12"

FLOWER COLOR: *E. giganteum* (blue-gray), *E. planum* (blue)

FLOWERING PERIOD: July

ZONES: *E. giganteum* (4–8), *E. planum* (5–9)

Most of the 200 species of *Eryngium* are native to either the Americas or the Mediterranean region. The common name sea holly refers to their often spiny leaves and the occurrence of many species in coastal areas. They have dense, cone-shaped flower heads surrounded by large, finely cut bracts. The most desirable eryngiums for drying have blue or blue-gray flowers.

E. giganteum is one of the most spectacular of the sea hollies. It can grow to a height of 5 feet, with flower heads 4 inches across. The broad floral bracts overlap to form an impressive blue-gray cup. The flowering stalks are well branched and produce many heads of varying sizes. Short-lived perennials, the plants often die after flowering but self-seed readily.

E. planum, by contrast, has flowers less than 1 inch wide, but they are produced in abundance and are a nice, bright blue color.

The flower heads of both species are ready to pick when they are at their peak of color, often as the tiny stamens are beginning to show in the florets, giving the heads a fuzzy appearance. The heads on each flowering stalk mature at different times and can be picked separately. This is an easy matter with *E. giganteum* but very tedious with the many small flowers of *E. planum*. As a compromise, you may pick flowering stalks of the latter when most of the heads are mature and hang them upside down to dry. Heads of either species picked separately can be dried loose on a wire screen or in a basket. and later attached to false stems (see page 28).

Sea hollies do best in deep, well-drained soil but can tolerate poor (though not wet) conditions. Full sunlight is essential to bring out the brightest-colored flowers.

E. giganteum

E. planum

Eryngium species

GOMPHRENA SPECIES

GLOBE AMARANTH

**TENDER ANNUAL,
TENDER PERENNIAL**

PROPAGATION: seeds

HEIGHT: 24"

**PLANTING
DISTANCE:** 10"

FLOWER COLOR:
white, pink, rose, lavender,
purple, red, orange

FLOWERING PERIOD:
July–frost

The globe amaranth, like its distant relatives the true amaranths, are primarily tropical plants that grows best in abundant warmth and sunshine. A good soil is also essential, and plants benefit greatly from applications of composted manure.

Two species are commonly grown as everlastings. Both are erect, well-branched plants that bloom profusely throughout the summer and autumn. The flower heads, which bear a superficial resemblance to clover blossoms, are composed of tiny florets surrounded by chaffy colored bracts. Globe amaranths are among the most frequently visited nectar plants of a wide range of butterflies.

Gomphrena globosa is a tender annual with flowers in shades of white, rose, pinks, and purple. Some relatively new cultivars, such as 'Lavender Lady', are an intense lavender-rose.

G. haageana is a herbaceous perennial in its native Mexico but must be grown as an annual where freezing temperatures occur. Its flowers, borne on relatively long, straight stems, are either bright red or orange.

Pick the flower heads of both species when they are at their peak of color and before the bracts surrounding the lower florets begin to turn brown. Heads picked too late will shatter easily after drying. Bunch the stems and hang upside down to dry.

G. globosa
'Lavender Lady'

G. haageana
'Strawberry Fields'

Gomphrena globosa

GRASSES

PROPAGATION: seeds

HEIGHT: *L. ovatus* (18"),
P. canariensis (36"), *S. italica*
(48"), *H. jubatum* (24")

**PLANTING
DISTANCE:** *H. jubatum*,
12", other (annuals), 1–2"

FLOWER COLOR: green

FLOWERING PERIOD:
*L. ovatus, P. canariensis,
H. jubatum* (June–July),
S. italica
(August–September)

ZONES: *H. jubatum* (7–10)

There are more than 7000 species of grasses in the world, and with so many to choose from, you know that there must be a few which are excellent everlastings.

Bunny's-tail grass, *Lagurus ovatus*, is aptly named for the shape and soft texture of the flower heads, which are pale green with an occasional hint of pink. This species, a small annual, grows in tufts just 18 inches tall.

Canary grass, *Phalaris canariensis*, another annual, has stiff, papery, green-and-white variegated heads and grows to a height of 3 feet. The seeds are an important component of the feed of cage birds.

The tallest grass that we grow is foxtail millet, *Setaria italica*. This annual reaches a height of 4 feet and has fat, bristly, spikelike flower heads. It is spectacular when planted in a large clump or block. The young heads are bright green and mature to golden brown.

The other "animal tail" that we grow is squirreltail grass, *Hordeum jubatum*. The heads of this half-hardy perennial have long, spreading, pink-tinged awns (bristles) that make them look as wide as they are long. A large clump of this grass is attractive in the flower garden, but it will self-seed in abundance if the flower heads are not removed.

Pick all of the grasses just as the heads are maturing but while they are still green. Most grasses shatter easily if picked later, but foxtail millet holds together well even if picked when brown. Squirreltail grass is especially prone to shattering and should be picked just as the awns are beginning to spread out from the head. Hang grasses upside down to dry.

Wild birds are fond of the seeds of canary grass and foxtail millet. Leave some in the garden for their fall and winter foraging, or pick some

Hordeum jubatum

Setaria italica

Lagurus ovatus

bunches after their seeds have matured and hang them up by your bird feeder.

Sow the seeds of annual grasses in rows in the garden. The seedlings need not be thinned. Squirreltail grass can be started either indoors or out in the garden. Grow it as an annual in areas colder than USDA Zone 7.

Many other grasses are worth growing as everlastings, including members of the genera *Briza* and *Chasmanthium*.

Hordeum jubatum, Setaria italica, and Phalaris canariensis

GYPSOPHILA PANICULATA

HARDY PERENNIAL

PROPAGATION: stem cuttings

HEIGHT: 36"

PLANTING DISTANCE: 18"

FLOWER COLOR: white, pink

FLOWERING PERIOD: July

ZONES: 3–9

The genus *Gypsophila* contains the many plants which are commonly called baby's-breath. The only one worth drying, however, is *G. paniculata*, a hardy plant that branches profusely and bears masses of midsummer blossoms. The largest and most double flowers are the most desirable, as these will retain the best size and color when dried.

Although seeds for double varieties are available, the best flowers are obtained from cultivars that do not produce seed and are therefore propagated asexually. Commercial nurseries propagate this species by tissue culture, but home gardeners can root stem cuttings taken in early summer. The most popular cultivars are 'Bristol Fairy' and 'Perfecta'. White is the most common color, but pink is also available.

Baby's-breath is best picked as soon as the flowers are fully open. If picked too early, they will be very small when dried. If picked too late, they will discolor. Unfortunately, only some of the flowers on a stalk will mature at a given time. We usually cut 10-inch stalks of flowers after most of them have opened. The flowers remaining on the plant will open later, yielding additional cuttings. Hang the flower stalks upside down to dry.

Baby's-breath is susceptible to root rot; choose a well-drained site and don't overwater.

G. p. 'Bristol Fairy'

Gypsophila paniculata

HELICHRYSUM BRACTEATUM

PERENNIAL, GROWN AS ANNUAL

PROPAGATION: seeds

HEIGHT: 60"

PLANTING DISTANCE: 10"

FLOWER COLOR: orange, pink, purple, red, white, yellow

FLOWERING PERIOD: July–frost

The strawflower, a native of Australia, has been a garden favorite for centuries. Although dwarf varieties are now available, *Helichrysum bracteatum* 'Monstrosum' is a giant, often exceeding 6 feet in height. It is a profuse bloomer that will flower throughout the summer.

Pick the flower buds as soon as they have opened their outermost bracts but before the center of the flower is showing. If picked later, the buds will open up completely during drying and be unattractive. Strawflowers are most often mounted on wires as they have a heavy flower head and a weak stem. You can attach a wire to the flower without tape if you do it soon after picking. First, cut off all but 1/4 inch of the stem, then pass a 22-gauge wire through the stem up into the flower head. As the flower head dries, it will shrink and tighten onto the wire. Flowers on wires can be dried upright, but hang those on natural stems upside down to dry.

Strawflowers are susceptible to root and stem rot and must be grown in well-drained soil.

H. bracteatum

Helichrysum bracteatum

HELIPTERUM SPECIES

HALF-HARDY ANNUAL,
TENDER ANNUAL

PROPAGATION: seeds

HEIGHT: 18"

PLANTING
DISTANCE: 10"

FLOWER COLOR:
H. roseum (white, pink),
H. humboldtianum (golden
yellow)

FLOWERING PERIOD:
June–July

*H*elipterum is another genus native primarily to Australia which includes some excellent everlastings. Although most members of the genus are tender plants, the acrocliniums, *H. roseum,* can tolerate near-freezing temperatures and even some light frost. The stout, well-branched plants produce many flowers on single 10-inch stems. The flowers resemble daisies, with bright yellow centers and white or pink petallike bracts.

If the flower buds are picked just before they are fully open, they will open perfectly while drying. If picked after they have opened, the colored bracts will turn back and the yellow centers blacken. If picked while still tightly closed, the buds will open only slightly while drying.

The Humboldt sunray, *H. humboldtianum,* is a well-branched, though somewhat floppy plant. The tiny golden yellow flower heads grow in tight clusters and must also be picked just before they open. The first flower cluster to mature is usually 2 to 3 inches in diameter. Buds farther down the stalk will yield smaller clusters later on.

Hang the flowers of both helipterums upside down to dry.

Both helipterums should be grown in a good, moist soil in full sunlight.

H. roseum

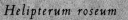

Helipterum roseum

LAVANDULA SPECIES

**HARDY PERENNIAL,
TENDER PERENNIAL**

PROPAGATION:
cuttings

HEIGHT: 12–48"

**PLANTING
DISTANCE:** *L. angustifolia*
cvs. (18"), *L. x intermedia*
cvs. (24")

FLOWER COLOR:
L. angustifolia cvs. (calyx:
violet-blue, corolla: white,
pink, violet), *L. x intermedia*
cvs. (calyx: gray-green,
corolla: white, violet)

FLOWERING PERIOD:
L. angustifolia cvs. (late
June–early July), *L. x
intermedia* cvs. (late July,
late September)

ZONES: 5–10

Few nonfood plants have had such a long and intimate association with humanity as the lavenders. Natives of the Mediterranean region, they were favorites of the Greeks and Romans. The latter used the flowers to scent their baths, and the name lavender has its origin in the Latin *lavo*, which means "I wash."

Along with about twenty species of *Lavandula*, a large number of cultivars and hybrids offer a range of flower colors, leaf shapes and textures, and growth habits. For drying, the best are the English lavenders, *Lavandula angustifolia* cvs. and the lavandins, *L.* × *intermedia* cvs., the latter being hybrids between the English lavenders and spike lavender, *L. latifolia*.

Lavender flowers consist of a tubular calyx and a longer tubular corolla, which are packed into dense spikes. Because only the calyces persist after drying, consider their color when choosing varieties for this purpose.

Cultivars of *L. angustifolia* produce the deepest violet-purple calyces. These include 'Hidcote', 'Loddon Blue', and 'Royal Purple'. Most English lavenders are compact shrubs between 18 and 24 inches tall, and most bloom once, in early summer. Some cultivars, such as 'Sharon Roberts', have a second flush of bloom in early autumn.

The calyx color of the lavandins is green-gray with just a hint of violet. Though not very colorful as dried flowers, they are very fragrant and productive and will yield at least two good crops in areas with a long growing season. The flower spikes are longer and thicker than those of the English lavenders and are carried on stems up to 20 inches tall, making them excellent material for lavender wands, or dollies.

Lavandin plants tend to be taller, with some, such as 'Grappenhall', reaching a height of 4 feet. 'Grosso' is more compact, 'Hidcote Giant' has

L. angustifolia
'Hidcote'

L. angustifolia cv.

L. angustifolia cv.

perhaps the largest flower spikes, and 'Dutch' has exceptionally gray foliage.

Harvest all of the lavenders and lavandins just as the first few florets are opening in the spikes. As not all of the spikes on a plant will mature simultaneously, you must either painstakingly pick each mature spike separately or harvest all of the spikes on a plant when the majority are ready. Bunch the stems and hang them upside down to dry.

All lavenders require full sun and a well-drained soil. Mulching with organic matter and manuring heavily are not advisable because they encourage fungal diseases. Both lavenders and lavandins can be propagated by cuttings taken in late summer. The English lavenders produce seeds (the lavandins are sterile), which need moist-chilling (see page 17) to germinate. However, the seedlings will be quite variable; rooting cuttings is the way we recommend to increase particular cultivars.

Several *Lavandula* cultivars

LIMONIUM SPECIES

**HARDY PERENNIAL,
HALF-HARDY
PERENNIAL, ANNUAL**

PROPAGATION: seeds

HEIGHT: L. latifolium,
L. perezii (20"),
L. sinuatum (24")

**PLANTING
DISTANCE:** L. latifolium,
L. perezii (10"), L. sinuatum,
(12")

FLOWER COLOR:
L. latifolium (white and
lavender), L. perezii (violet-
purple), L. sinuatum apricot,
lavender, pink, purple,
white, yellow

FLOWERING PERIOD:
L. latifolium, L. perezii,
(July–August), L. sinuatum
(July–frost)

ZONES: 3–9

The genus *Limonium* comprises about 150 species, several of which make good everlastings. *L. latifolium*, commonly called sea lavender, is a hardy perennial at home along the eastern coast of the Mediterranean Sea. From a crown of wide, smooth, and leathery basal leaves, several tall, graceful sprays of tiny flowers are produced in midsummer. Each floret consists of a lavender corolla surrounded by a papery white calyx.

Annual statice, *L. sinuatum*, another Mediterranean native, forms a clump of basal leaves and numerous flowering stalks. The flowers, which are arranged in graceful, arching clusters, consist of small, cream-colored corollas and cuplike calyces in many bright colors which cannot be found in any of the other everlastings. The corollas wither and fall off during drying, leaving the colorful calyces to become the dried flowers.

The more tender *L. perezii* is native to the Canary Islands. Its foliage is similar to sea lavender, but the violet-purple calyces and white corollas are much larger and more akin to those of the annual statice. It can be grown as an annual in areas colder than zone 8.

Pick sprays of *L. latifolium* when most of its flower are open. The corollas will shrivel but remain to add a touch of color to the dried calyces. You may dry the flower sprays upright. The tiny white-and-lavender dried flowers on graceful, curving stems make this a light and delicate everlasting.

Pick flowering stalks of *L. perezii* and *L. sinuatum* after all of the calyces and a few of the petals are open. Bunch the stalks and hang them upside down to dry.

Grow limoniums in a deep, well-drained soil. The plants do not like to have their roots disturbed, so it is best to propagate the perennials as well as the annuals from seeds rather than division.

L. latifolium

L. sinuatum

Limonium sinuatum. The sprig at lower left has been preserved in glycerine.

LUNARIA ANNUA

HARDY BIENNIAL

PROPAGATION: seeds

HEIGHT: 36"

PLANTING DISTANCE: 10"

FLOWER COLOR: flowers purple or white, pods white

FLOWERING PERIOD: May

ZONES: 4–8

Lunaria annua is a European native common throughout the world as a fragrant garden flower and as an excellent everlasting. It has accumulated a truly cosmopolitan list of common names, such as money plant, moonwort, Pope's money, and satin flower. All refer to the plant's most distinguishing feature, the shiny, silvery, translucent membrane partitioning the flat, round seedpod.

Each plant produces a single tall, well-branched flowering stalk bearing small purple or white flowers. Harvest the entire stalk after all of its flowers have turned into papery seedpods. The shiny inner membrane is revealed by peeling off the two outer "shells" of the pod. Save the outer coverings for use as false petals when you make pinecone flowers.

The plant is the only everlasting in this book which prefers a shady location. If you don't harvest all of the seedpods, the plants will self-seed readily.

L. annua

Lunaria annua

Nigella species

LOVE-IN-MIST • FENNEL FLOWER

HARDY ANNUALS

PROPAGATION: seeds

HEIGHT: *N. damascena*
(20"), *N. hispanica* (16"),
N. orientalis (24")

**PLANTING
DISTANCE:** 6"

FLOWER COLOR:
N. damascena (white, blue,
rose), *N. hispanica* (violet-
blue), *N. orientalis* (yellow)

FLOWERING PERIOD:
June–July and beyond

*N*igella is a small genus of Mediterranean annual herbs. The common names fennel flower and love-in-a-mist refer to their somewhat fennellike foliage and to the appearance of their flowers, which are surrounded by a mist of finely divided, leafy bracts.

The often brightly colored flowers are short-lived. As soon as their petallike sepals fall, however, the inflated ovaries form striking seedpods, which dry exceedingly well. Persistent pronglike styles extending from the tops of the pods add greatly to their visual effect.

N. damascena is an attractive garden flower that can become a pesky weed if allowed to self-seed. The white, blue, or rose flowers are semidouble, and the green pods bear a beautiful pattern of vertical rose-purple stripes.

By contrast, *N. hispanica* is a sprawling plant with coarser foliage and larger, bolder violet-blue flowers punctuated by deep maroon-red stamens. The pods are a subdued tan-green, but the styles are long and flare sharply outward.

N. orientalis is the least showy of these three species. Its flowers are an inconspicuous yellow and the pods, a pale tan-green. Yet these compact pods often lend a perfect subtle touch to a floral design.

Nigella pods are ready to harvest when they are papery and firm to the touch. If left too long on the plants, the colors will fade and turn brown. Dry them upright or hang upside down to dry.

Plant seeds directly outdoors in early spring. Full sunlight is best for all three species.

N. damascena

Nigella damascena

ORIGANUM SPECIES

**HARDY, HALF-HARDY,
TENDER PERENNIALS**

PROPAGATION:
cuttings, division
(*O. vulgare* ssp. *vulgare*, *O.
rotundifolium* 'Kent Beauty'),
seeds (*O. rotundifolium*)

HEIGHT: *O. rotundifolium*
(6"), *O. vulgare* ssp. *vulgare*
(24"), *O. calcaratum* x (6"),
O. dictamnus (12")

**PLANTING
DISTANCE:** 10"

FLOWER COLOR: rose-
green, purple

FLOWERING PERIOD:
July–August

ZONES: *O. calcaratum*
(8–10), *O. dictamnus* (10),
O. laevigatum (7–10), *O.
libanoticum* (7–10), *O.
rotundifolium* (7–10), *O.
vulgare* ssp. *vulgare* (4–8)

*O*riganum is a relatively small genus native to the Mediterranean region and central Asia. Many species have been valued as cooking and healing herbs for thousands of years, yet only in the past few decades have they found wide acceptance in the ornamental garden.

Origanum flowers have tiny corollas, but they are surrounded by larger, often colorful bracts which dry extremely well. The most common and productive origanum for dried flowers is the herb known as wild marjoram, *O. vulgare* ssp. *vulgare*. Its leaves are virtually tasteless, but they are still used today in medicinal preparations. The subspecies is very variable, and its flower spikelets, set in heads 2 inches across, range in color from pale greenish pink to deep purple. It is easily grown from seeds, but the flower colors of the seedling will vary greatly. As with the lavenders and yarrows, it is best to select plants which have been propagated asexually.

Several less hardy origanums are excellent for the rockery, small garden, or containers and also yield interesting dried flowers. *O. rotundifolium* grows a scant 6 inches high and has round, scentless, leathery leaves. Its large, bright green bracts overlap like those of hops. A choice cultivar is 'Kent Beauty', with bright rose bracts.

Dittany of Crete, *O. dictamnus*, is a small, semitrailing plant perfect for pot culture. Its fuzzy gray-green leaves are most attractive and make a nice tea. A hybrid of recent origin often sold as showy dittany is a profuse bloomer with more colorful bracts and is a bit hardier.

Some other origanums to try include *O. calcaratum*, which resembles a taller dittany of Crete, *O. libanoticum*, with long, pendulous rose-green bracts, and *O. laevigatum*, which has wiry, upright stems and relatively small purple

O. vulgare ssp.
vulgare

O. rotundifolium
'Kent Beauty'

Several ornamental *Origanums*

bracts. Hybrids with brightly colored floral bracts include 'Ray Williams', 'Nancy Wilson', and 'Hopleys'.

Pick all of the origanums at their peak of color before the the older bracts begin to turn brown. Hang upside down to dry. We have preserved the leafy stems of *O. rotundifolium* with glycerin (see page 26), which keeps them soft and pliable but turns them a tan color.

A well-drained soil is essential, as some species are susceptible to root rot in wet, humid conditions. Wild marjoram, however, seems adaptable almost anywhere. Full sun is preferred to bring out the color of the bracts.

All origanums can be propagated by cuttings. 'Kent Beauty', which sends out underground stems, and wild marjoram, which suckers from a woody base, are easy to divide. *O. rotundifolium* can also be grown from seeds.

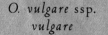

O. vulgare ssp.
vulgare

Origanum laevigatum and *O. vulgare ssp. vulgare*

Papaver somniferum

HARDY ANNUAL

PROPAGATION: seeds

HEIGHT: 3–4'

PLANTING DISTANCE: 10"

FLOWER COLOR:
white, lavender, red, pink

FLOWERING PERIOD:
June

Here is a plant that has provided humanity with beautiful flowers for the garden, admirable seedpods for floral designs, edible seeds for cooking, and essential sedatives and painkillers for medicine. Unfortunately, it has been sorely abused for its narcotic properties and is little known by most gardeners. The poppy seeds of commerce, by the way, which come from this species, are safe to eat and do not contain narcotic substances. The erect plants, which grow to 4 feet high, bear smooth gray-green leaves. The flowers are quite variable. The petals may be white, pink, lavender, or red, often with a splotch of dark purple at the base of each one. Plant breeders have introduced varieties with more numerous petals, giving the flowers the appearances of a cheerleader's pompons and giving rise to the name peony poppy.

The immature pods are green, turning lavender-gray as they ripen and harden. The opening of pores under the cap of each mature pod is an indication that it is ready to harvest. When you pick the pods, shake the seeds into a clean container for later use in baking. Strip the leaves from the cut stems and dry the stems upright in a container.

A cultivar called 'Hens and Chicks' has a large central seedpod surrounded at its base by numerous small, partly developed pods. Their visual effect is dramatic. Pores of this cultivar do not open, however, and so you must cut the pods open to release the seeds. Pick the pods when they are hard and firm to the touch.

Plant seeds of opium poppy directly outdoors, either in late fall or early spring. Choose a spot with full sun and moist soil. Plants thinned to stand at least 10 inches apart and well fertilized will yield the largest pods.

P. somniferum

P. s. 'Hens & Chicks'

Papaver somniferum and *P.s.* 'Hens and Chicks'

83

SALVIA SPECIES

**HALF-HARDY
PERENNIALS**

PROPAGATION:
cuttings, seeds
(*S. farinacea*)

HEIGHT: 36–48"

**PLANTING
DISTANCE:** *S. farinacea*
(12"), *S. leucantha* (18–24")

FLOWER COLOR:
S. farinacea (violet-blue),
S. leucantha (purple)

FLOWERING PERIOD:
S. farinacea
(June–September),
S. leucantha (August)

ZONES: *S. farinacea*
(8–10), *S. leucantha* (9–10)

*S*alvia is a large, worldwide genus containing more than 750 species. Their often colorful flowers and fragrant foliage have made them garden favorites, and many herbs are included in their ranks. Hummingbirds find the long tubular flowers of several species irresistible as nectar sources. Some sages are also attractive everlastings.

Mealy-cup sage, *S. farinacea,* is a half-hardy perennial that is often grown as an annual. The cultivar 'Blue Bedder' is well branched to a height of 4 feet and blooms throughout the summer and autumn. Both the calyces and corollas on the long flower spike are a deep violet-blue, but as with the lavenders, only the calyces persist after drying. Dried spikes of this sage even resemble those of the English lavenders, but they are larger and thicker and lack the lavender's wonderful fragrance.

Mexican bush sage, *S. leucantha,* is another large, prolific bloomer. It is a tender perennial, but it can be grown in colder climates from small cuttings or plants which have been wintered over indoors. The showy flowers have soft purple calyces and either white or purple corollas. The latter form is a cultivar aptly named 'All Purple'. Because again only the calyces persist, both types yield purple dried flowers, but the color is brighter in 'All Purple'.

Harvest both sages when the first few corollas on each spike begin to open. Bunch the spikes and hang them upside down to dry.

Grow both sages in full sun and a well-drained soil. The seeds of *S. farinacea* are treated either as for perennials or hardy annuals that are started indoors.

S. farinacea
'Blue Bedder Sage'

S. leucantha
'All Purple'

Salvia farinacea

Scabiosa stellata

HARDY ANNUAL

PROPAGATION: seeds

HEIGHT: 20"

PLANTING DISTANCE: 10"

FLOWER COLOR: pale lavender-pink (fresh), green (dried)

FLOWERING PERIOD: July

Starflower is an old-fashioned garden plant native to the western Mediterranean region, appreciation for which has only recently been revived. It is a hardy, well-branched annual with hairy, toothed leaves and many spherical heads of pale lavender-pink blossoms. When the petals of each flower fall, they reveal a persistent starlike center in a delicately striped, cuplike calyx. Despite its neutral, green-gray color, it makes a striking and unusual dried flower.

Pick the flower heads as soon as the last few petals have fallen off. If picked too early, they will shrivel when dried. If picked too late, the heads are likely to shatter. Dry the flower heads upright. Even when picked properly, the dried flowers are very delicate. Spraying the heads with an aerosol glue will help to hold them together. Preserving the flower heads with glycerin (see page 26) makes them almost shatterproof but also turns them a less attractive brown color.

S. stellata

Scabiosa stellata

Xeranthemum annuum

HARDY ANNUAL

PROPAGATION: seeds

HEIGHT: 24"

**PLANTING
DISTANCE:** 10"

FLOWER COLOR:
white, rose, purple

FLOWERING PERIOD:
July–frost

The immortelle is a neat, bushy plant which blooms freely from midsummer until the first frost. You'll probably need only a few plants as each one will produce more than a hundred blossoms. The papery flowers look like daisies, and some smell like wintergreen. They come in single and double forms, in white, rose, and purple. All make superb, though fragile, dried flowers.

Pick the flowers when they are fully open but before they discolor or produce seeds. Dried unopened flower buds are also attractive in small bouquets and arrangements.

Bunch the stems and hang them upside down to dry. They are easily crushed and are best stored as hanging bunches rather than in boxes.

X. annuum

Xeranthemum annuum

ADDITIONAL FLOWERS/PODS FOR DRYING

Plant Name	When to Harvest	Flower/Pod Colors	Life Cycle
Anaphalis margaritacea pearly everlasting	2	white	HP
Asclepias tuberosa butterfly weed	1	tan	HP
Baptisia australis false indigo	1/G	black/brown	HP
Carlina aucalis carline thistle	2	silver/white	HP
Chrysanthemum parthenium feverfew	2	beige/white	HP
Helichrysum thianshanicum golden baby	2	yellow	HP
Hydrangea macrophylla bigleaf hydrangea	2	green, pink, blue	HS
Leontopodium alpinum edelweiss	2	gray/white	HP
Lonas annua African daisy	2	yellow	HHA
Marrubium incanum silver horehound	5	green	HP
Molucella laevis bells of Ireland	2/G	tan	HA
Monarda citriodora lemon beebalm	5	lavender	HA

K E Y

When to Harvest

1   when the seed pod is fully formed
2   when the flower(s) is fully formed
3   when the flower is a tight bud
4   when the flower bud is semi-open
5   when the petals have fallen from the flower head
6   pick the leafy stems
G   preserve with glycerin

Plant Name	When to Harvest	Flower/Pod Colors	Life Cycle
Monarda didyma beebalm	1	brown	HP
Nepeta cataria catnip	5	green	HP
Paeonia hybrids peony	2	pink/red	HP
Physalis alkekengi Chinese lanterns	1	orange	HP
Psylliostachys suworowii Russian statice	2	pink	HA
Pycnanthemum pilosum mountain mint	5	green/pink	HP
Rosa ssp. rose	3	pink, red, yellow	HS
Ruta graveolens rue	1	tan, green	HS
Santolina ssp. santolina	2	yellow	HS
Senecio cineraria dusty miller	6	silver/gray	HP
Stachys lanata lamb's ears	3	silver/gray	HP
Tanacetum vulgare tansy	2	yellow	HP

Life Cycle

HA	hardy annual
HP	hardy perennial
HS	hardy shrub
HHA	half-hardy annual

SELECTED SOURCES

The Flowery Branch, PO Box 1330, Flowery Branch, GA 30542

Goodwin Creek Gardens, PO Box 83, Williams, OR 97544

Nichols Garden Nursery, 1190 N. Pacific Hwy., Albany, OR 97321-4598

Park Seed Co., Cokesbury Rd., Greenwood, SC 29647-0001

Richters, Goodwood, ON L0C 1A0, Canada

Pinetree Garden Seeds, Rt. 100, New Gloucester, ME 04260

Thompson and Morgan, PO Box 1308, Jackson, NJ 08527-0308

RECOMMENDED READING

Armitage, Allen. *Specialty Cut Flowers.* Portland, Oregon: Timber Press, 1993. Covers both fresh and dried flowers, and is geared primarily to commercial—but has helpful information to the home gardener.

Bailey, L. H. *How Plants Get Their Names.* New York: Dover, 1963. This is a delightful book which contains a good Latin-English dictionary of botanical names.

Bradley, Fern, and Barbara Ellis, eds. *Encyclopedia of Organic Gardening.* Emmaus, Pennsylvania: Rodale Press, 1992. This large book clearly explains all aspects of organic gardening.

Coombes, Allen J. *Dictionary of Plant Names.* Portland, Oregon: Timber Press, 1985. This is another book that explains the derivation of botanical names.

Hillier, Malcolm, and Colin Hilton. *The Book of Dried Flowers.* New York: Simon and Schuster, 1986. An excellent source of ideas for crafting with dried flowers.

Jeavons, John. *How to Grow More Vegetables.* Palo Alto, California: Ecology Action of the Mid-Peninsula, 1974. This book explains the biodynamic/French intensive method of organic gardening, especially useful for people with a small garden space.

Pulleyn, Rob. *The Wreath Book.* New York: Sterling, 1988. Basic wreath design, with a wealth of examples for every occasion.

Reader's Digest Association, eds. *Reader's Digest Illustrated Guide to Gardening.* Pleasantville, New York, 1978. This is a comprehensive and well-illustrated guide to gardening. It includes excellent plant lists for a variety of purposes.

I N D E X